K.E.E.P.
P.E.D.A.L.I.N.G.

THE THINGS I LEARNED ON MY BIKE

KARON JOSEPH RILEY

Keep Pedaling: The Things I Learned On My Bike
Copyright 2023 by Karon Joseph Riley.

All rights reserved. No part of this publication may be reproduced, distributed, or transmitted in any form or by any means, including photocopying, recording, or other electronic or mechanical methods, without the prior written permission of the publisher, except in the case of brief quotations embodied in critical reviews and certain other noncommercial uses permitted by copyright law.

For permission requests, write to the publisher, addressed "Attention: Permissions Coordinator," 205 N. Michigan Avenue, Suite #810, Chicago, IL 60601. 13th & Joan books may be purchased for educational, business or sales promotional use. For information, please email the Sales Department at sales@13thandjoan.com.

Printed in the U. S. A.

First Printing, March 2024

Library of Congress Cataloging-in-Publication Data has been applied for.

ISBN: 978-1-961863-03-3

*I dedicate this to my mother
for making me believe in myself
without the shadow of a doubt
and to my ancestors who Kept Pedaling
so I too will Keep Pedaling.
Asè*

FOREWORD

The author of the book you are holding is a young man who has been successful in not one extremely difficult profession but two, where only one percent succeed. He played football in the NFL long enough to earn a pension and has become a successful working actor. He is now attempting to become a triple hyphenate by becoming a successful author with his first book. I invite you to join him as he shares with his readers his philosophy on becoming a two-time one percenter and how to stay the course when it is so much easier just to quit. In other words, just Keep Pedaling.

— Fred J. Riley Jr.

CONTENTS

Foreword v

Prologue 1

Introduction 3

Chapter 1: K | Knowledge................7

Chapter 2: E | Experience 13

Chapter 3: E | Evolve 19

Chapter 4: P | Purpose....................25

Chapter 5: P | Pray..........................29

Chapter 6: E | Elevate 37

Chapter 7: D | Discipline 43

Chapter 8: A | Accountability..........51

Chapter 9: L | Leadership...............59

Chapter 10: I | Integrity 67

Chapter 11: N | Navigate................75

Chapter 12: G | Give 83

Personal Quotes 89

My Peloton (My Village) 91

Epilogue..103

Acknowledgments 105

About the Author 111

PROLOGUE

K.E.E.P P.E.D.A.L.I.N.G.

The book is broken down by the mantra of K.E.E.P. P.E.D.A.L.I.N.G. Each letter has meaning and will be followed by 10 proverbs or wise quotes from multiple sources. I'll break down what each means to me and why it matters to the overall energy required to Keep Pedaling. It's not a brand, it's an energy. Get you some!

INTRODUCTION

Growing up, my father, brother, cousins, and coaches always taught me lessons. Each one seemed to come with a rule or clause in that rule that could never be broken or changed. For example, after my brother taught me how to throw a baseball and then a football, that lesson was followed up with the comment, *"Every man should know how to throw any kind of ball properly."* Never mind that my brother himself was a teenager at the time and not yet a man. He was a man to me at the young age of 4. Shortly after that lesson, I got the lesson of learning to ride my bike. That lesson was and is probably one of the best attained skills I've ever obtained because it brought my first taste of freedom. Freedom is to a person what water is to a fish. We gotta have it, feel it, control it. On that bike, I started to use my freedom to go out into the world and test my ever-growing library of man laws, as I called them, and to find and figure out some of my own laws for myself. On my bike, I could always think and stoke my imagination, albeit at that age my freedom only extended up and down my block. But as a kid, a block might as well be the whole world.

Throughout my growing up and accomplishing some pretty cool things, I've always found solace on my bike. Even now, when I have a problem I can't quite crack, a good long bike ride usually unravels the knot for me. It helps me to see my life from a bird's eye view and actually pull the lessons of my life out and into the waking world. As I work through the many obstacles life throws at me, I find myself remembering a lot of the experiences and knowledge my life has afforded me. I'm then able to apply those already programmed rules into whatever algorithm my spirit is sorting through. This book is in essence a map and chart of my internal wisdom that the world I have created and lived in has invested in me. The very mantra I live by of Keep Pedaling came from a bike ride at a time when I felt the most lost. The answer the Most High sent to me was to Keep Pedaling no matter the speed. Never stopping is the only way through the problem and back home. As I rode and rode, I developed a template that when life challenges me outside of my comfort zone, I have a foundation of rules and wisdom that I can plug and play accordingly. This is my way of helping somebody to help themselves, for I understand that the only person who will save us is us by applying the wisdom within us.

As you read this personal manifesto of my own operating system, I hope there is something that you can add to yours that will help you endure and evolve to be your greatest self. One of my favorite poems is authored by Marianne Williamson.

OUR DEEPEST FEAR

Our deepest fear is not that we are inadequate. Our deepest fear is that we are powerful beyond measure. It is our light, not our darkness, that most frightens us.

We ask ourselves, 'Who am I to be brilliant, gorgeous, talented, fabulous?' Actually, who are you not to be? You are a child of God.

Your playing small does not serve the world. There is nothing enlightened about shrinking so that other people won't feel insecure around you.

We are all meant to shine, as children do. We were born to make manifest the glory of God that is within us.

It's not just in some of us; it's in everyone.

And as we let our own light shine, we unconsciously give other people permission to do the same. As we are liberated from our own fear, our presence automatically liberates others.

This is my attempt at shining my little light on the world so that you may also shine your light and Keep Pedaling onward and upward.

CHAPTER 1

KNOWLEDGE

Knowledge:
Facts, information, and skills acquired by a person through experience or education; the theoretical or practical understanding of a subject.

Until the lion learns how to write, every story will glorify the hunter.

— African Proverb

THE LESSON

I believe the first letter of K.E.E.P. P.E.D.A.L.I.N.G. is for knowledge. I believe that knowledge in itself is powerful, but self-knowledge is definitely a superpower. I'm not talking about knowledge of self, such as where you were born and your favorite food and color. I'm speaking of the deepest knowledge of self–from your blood type to as many ancestors you can trace and find. Self-knowledge goes as deep as knowing what your great-grandparents did for a living. What genetic weaknesses lie in your history? Why should you or I care about how a relative who lived 100 years ago matters to what we are doing now? The world isn't anything like it was before, right? Well, I say that it matters because as an Afrikan man living on a soil that once not as long ago as it may seem, my ancestors were taken from our native land and planted here. They were subjected to some of the most heinous acts ever laid upon a human in the history of mankind. That connection is and always will be there, but so is the connection to a time when my people thrived.

Self-knowledge of one's complete history and culture has been proven to be beneficial beyond measure. The folks running this rat race understand this. This is why it's your imperative duty as a spirit living a human existence to seek, find, and consume the proper program for your reality. The bottom line is this: The great historian and ancestor Dr. John Henrik Clark said, *"People who don't know where they come from can be led anywhere."* So like a computer, we have to update our software (spirit) with the right programming so we can respond with the proper answers to our realities. So when I'm preparing for a long bike ride of 100 miles or more, I'll have the drivetrain checked and completely tuned up, and the tires and computers all changed and charged up. With me knowing I have done all of those things, my confidence to complete the journey is there, so my ability isn't far behind. For a life of 100 years or more—yes, I'm aiming for 120—you have to make sure your mind, spirit, and body can make the journey.

THE LAWS

1. Know thyself! The only elephant that can hurt you in the room is the elephant you don't know. This means we all have trauma. It can only hurt us when we don't acknowledge it.
2. To acquire knowledge one must study, but to acquire wisdom, one must observe. Study so you can see and pay attention to the signs all around you.
3. Knowledge becomes power only when we put it into use. Once you know better, you simply do better.
4. Knowledge is power. The more knowledge, expertise, and connections you have, the easier it is for you to make a profit at the game of your choice. Your net worth is your network.
5. Knowledge shared is power multiplied. There is nothing new under the sun or within the infinite intelligence, so sharing is caring.
6. Knowledge is when you learn something new every day. Wisdom is when you let something go every day. Stay open to the present. Observe, manage, and let go of the past.

7. True knowledge, according to Albert Einstein, comes with a deep understanding of a topic and its inner-workings. It is critical that we go so much deeper than surface information about ourselves. For example, you can't say you are vegan but you don't know your blood type.
8. The true sign of intelligence is not knowledge but imagination, according to Albert Einstein. It's your God-given right to be a co-creator of your life. What isn't seen is waiting to be manifested.
9. Knowledge is knowing a tomato is a fruit; wisdom is not putting it in a fruit salad, according to Miles Kington. Self-knowledge gives you situational awareness in all environments.
10. Knowledge is the true organ of sight, not the eyes, according to Panchatantra. Every answer for your life is internal.

THE REFLECTION

How can learning about the deepest parts of self help you manifest your dreams?

_____

_____

What is the first thing you will do to start learning about yourself?

_____

_____

What are three things you know and love about yourself? What are three things you don't like about yourself?

_____

_____

CHAPTER 2

EXPERIENCE

Experience:
The fact or state of having been affected by or gained knowledge through direct observation or participation.

Experiences are the spectacles of intellect.

— Nigerian Proverb

THE LESSON

Now we come to the place where the rubber meets the road. Have you ever heard the saying, *Life is the best teacher*? Well, that is a truth that can't be debated. Experience is one of the main tenets of my life, as it is yours, whether you acknowledge it or not. Hopefully after reading this, you will see and overstand that life doesn't happen to you but for you. Let's back up a bit and remember that knowledge is key. To be more specific, knowledge of self is the door, and experience is the key to unlocking said door. As I've grown and moved through life, I started to realize that everything that happened or happened to me is by design. It is by my design whether I see it in the moment or in hindsight. The key to experience is to understand that without it, nothing in your dreams or vision can be. Through experience, we learn how to deal with pain, loss, wins, love, anger, hate, and grief, just to name a few of the emotions that will hit you on your life journey. The people who can navigate these and much more will undoubtedly be successful in whatever they see for themselves.

THE LAWS

1. The purpose of life is to live it, to taste experience to the utmost, and to reach out eagerly without fear for newer and richer experiences, according to Eleanor Roosevelt. You came here to fully participate in the experience.
2. Every experience I have is perfect for my growth, according to Louise May. Life simply happens for me and not to me.
3. Fill your life with experiences, not things. Have stories to tell, not stuff to show. The richness is always in the moments.
4. Every experience is a positive experience if you view it as an opportunity for growth and self-mastery. Keep your glass half full always.
5. Experience is the hardest kind of teacher. It gives you the test first and the lesson afterward, according to Oscar Wilde. You only become brave once you face the fear.
6. Every experience in your life is being orchestrated to teach you something you need to know to move forward.

Ask for it and the universe will give. Just remember what you prayed for.
7. The only source of knowledge is experience, according to Albert Einstein. The only way is through.
8. Every experience makes you grow. Nothing on the planet has grown without darkness.
9. Nothing is a waste of time if you use the experience wisely. It's all a part of the plan.
10. There are no mistakes in life, only lessons. There is no such thing as a negative experience. There are only opportunities to grow, learn, and advance. Keep Pedaling.

THE REFLECTION

What have your life experiences taught you?

_____

_____

How have those experiences lined up with your dreams, your daily thoughts, and your actions?

_____

_____

How can you learn from your experiences to change and improve your life?

_____

_____

CHAPTER 3

EVOLVE

Evolve:
Develop gradually, especially from a simple to a more complex form

Either willfully evolve or let life force you to evolve.

— Karon Joseph Riley

THE LESSON

The second E in K.E.E.P.P.E.D.A.L.I.N.G. is going to happen whether you want it to or not. My way of evolving comes from a phrase I pulled out of the collective intelligence called "willful evolution." The definition is just like it sounds. Life will either force you to evolve through painful lessons or experiences, or you can willfully evolve based on you being honest with yourself about your shadows and your darkness. You will hear me say this over and over again. The elephants in the room can only hurt us if we fail to first acknowledge said elephants and go a step further and name the elephants, thus not allowing them to affect our outer lives. We all have them. They are created by trauma in some shape, fashion, or form. Whether it was something your parents did or didn't do, some bully, a coach, or a relative. This part is where we have to do the work. Go to therapy, talk to a professional who can help you sort these traumas out, and de-power them. Forgive yourself for the trauma happening to you. We always believe it was our fault when in actuality we are right, but our mindset has to shift to overstand that life happens for us, not to us.

In order for you and I to reach our highest elevation, we have to do the inner-work. The depth of our struggles will determine our success. We have to willfully evolve so we can control the narrative. Power versus force at all times. Evolution is a participatory event. You will be a part of it whether you acknowledge it or not. I implore you to always focus on yourself and your evolution from an introspective perspective. Success in life is definitely an inside job and if done right, you will actually get into a flow state of life. Challenges will come, yes. But as long as you take accountability for yourself, then your higher-self will always meet the challenge and come out of it, evolving into a better version of yourself.

THE LAWS

1. Either willfully evolve or have life force you to evolve. A hard head makes for a soft ass.
2. Evolving isn't just about changing. It's about growing wiser with each step. Don't waste time. Pay attention to signs so you don't have to repeat the lesson.
3. Embrace the pain of evolution, for it is the crucible of personal growth. Fire forges steel.
4. In the dance of life, those who evolve gracefully are the truest of artists. Keep your dancing shoes on rain or shine.
5. Don't fear change. It's the chisel that sculpts your better self.
6. Evolution is the silent teacher. Listen closely and you'll hear its profound lessons. Appreciate the silence. Sometimes it speaks the loudest.
7. Like a river carving through rock, time shapes us, but it's our choices that determine our course. Always know that without the shaping, you will never get smooth.

8. To evolve is to shed the old and embrace the new, like changing the tires on your bike. After every tire change, the ride feels really good.
9. In the tapestry of life, each thread of evolution adds depth and richness to the pattern. Nobody wants a boring sweater.
10. Life happens for you, not to you, according to Jay Z.

THE REFLECTION

Would you rather evolve willfully or by force? Why?

_____

_____

Do you see how you have evolved through your life thus far? Can you pinpoint evolution points?

_____

_____

Are you open to evolving to serve your purpose?

_____

_____

CHAPTER 4

PURPOSE

Purpose:
The reason or intention behind a particular action, decision, or existence. It represents a sense of direction, meaning, and fulfillment in one's life, often guiding one's goals and actions toward a specific aim or desired outcome. Having a sense of purpose provides individuals with a deeper understanding of their values, motivates them to pursue meaningful goals, and can contribute a greater sense of satisfaction and fulfillment in their lives.

Be on purpose about living your purpose.

— Karon Joseph Riley

THE LESSON

The fourth letter in the acronym is purpose. It is placed there because that is how you spell "keep," and also because most people won't discover their purpose without first acquiring knowledge of self and experiences and evolving by said knowledge and experiences. I myself personally didn't figure out my purpose until around 40. Now don't get me wrong, I always moved with purpose, but I didn't start moving on purpose until around 40. After 10 years of marriage and a ton of life experiences, which included having two children and successfully transitioning from one career to the next, I was able to understand my purpose. To be honest, it is an ever-moving guidepost. As I continue to evolve and experience and gain knowledge, my purpose evolves. But I truly overstand my direct purpose, which I believe is to move my culture into a more enlightened space through my creative gifts: To reach a level of awareness through my works as an artist, to be able to create a curiosity for my people, to obtain self-knowledge and awareness of our collective past so that we all can move into a more unified and stronger future for my children and the many generations to come.

Fredrick Douglas once said that knowledge makes a man unable to be a slave. My purpose for coming to the marketplace of the earth is to help my people free themselves from the oppressive world of tyranny we find ourselves in. Your quest to find your purpose is yours and yours alone. The result of that purpose will serve a much broader scope. We all must be able to stand on our own recognizance so that we can collectively hold up our own. I implore you to learn how to meditate and be still because in the quiet and dark, you will find the answers to your soul's purpose. I promise you that once you get to this point, you will be granted access to your God-power and from there, you will shine and start to manifest in ways that will feel like alchemy. Once you do, Keep Pedaling. Now you're getting the hang of it.

THE REFLECTION

What do you think your purpose is?

_____

_____

How do you think your purpose will serve the world?

_____

_____

How can you be on purpose about your purpose?

_____

_____

CHAPTER 5

PRAY

Prayer:
A form of communication with a higher power, deity, or a spiritual entity. It often involves spoken or silent words, thoughts, or rituals and is used for various purposes such as expressing gratitude, seeking guidance, requesting help, or offering praise and worship. Prayers can be religious or spiritual in nature and are an integral part of many cultures and belief systems worldwide.

Prayer is the song our ancestors sing to keep us safe and on our path.

— Afrikan Proverb

THE LESSON

There is an Afrikan proverb that says, *The left hand represents the past and the right hand represents the future. When you put them together in prayer, you are in the present.* That proverb makes so much sense to me because I believe our past, present, and future happen at the same time. Prayer to me when I was younger and not as enlightened by study and life was me literally talking to God outside of myself, which is how the system of life has been created to keep a middleman in between your true freedom and power. I've learned for myself that praying is definitely paramount to my success on this journey, not because I believe that I am speaking with something or someone external from me. I do believe I am speaking to God. The God in me, that is. What I've learned is we are all constantly praying with our thoughts, our words, our actions, which in turn creates the world we individually live in.

I remember when I was playing football from little league all the way up to the pros, I always said the same prayer: *Father protect Me.* I wrote positive quotes on my tape. I didn't quite understand like I do now but it worked, and now I overstand why it worked. I write down my goals (prayers) on my bathroom mirror. I do this because I truly believe once you write something with pen, it becomes its own energy and life that you as the god of your universe have the choice to raise to fruition or let it stay a spirit on that mirror or paper or whatever you have written your goals (prayers) down on. Everything you have written or seen in your mind's eye already exists in the collective consciousness of the world. The familiar bible passage of "there is nothing new under the sun" means that we are all connected to a higher level of conscience whether we know it or not. The people who overstand this have achieved amazing things.

So this is the cheat sheet of life. Guard your thoughts and your words. We are all powerful in our own right. If you think negative and speak negative, you're praying negative whether you are aware or not, and your outer world will reflect that negativity. So prayer is important, but what is more important is our understanding of prayer and realizing that you are always connected to the source so make sure you are paying attention to what you are praying for. When I go for bike rides, I always say a protection prayer over myself, thus reminding myself that my safety is my responsibility. My faith in connecting to the collective is that I feel whoever passes me has the same thought of safety for themselves and me indirectly.

THE LAWS

1. Prayer should be genuine and heartfelt, reflecting your true intentions and emotions. Be authentic in all you do.
2. Believing in the power of prayer and having faith in the entity or force you are praying to is essential. You have to believe before you can achieve.
3. Show respect and reverence when addressing the divine, using appropriate language and gestures based on your tradition. Humility is salvation.
4. Establish a consistent prayer routine to maintain a strong spiritual connection. Stay on purpose about your purpose.
5. Find a quiet, secluded place for personal prayers to minimize distractions and enhance focus. Silence is the secret to hearing the voice.
6. Express gratitude for your blessings and positive experiences. Gratitude invites blessings.
7. Request guidance, assistance, or forgiveness and understand that it has already happened. Walk by faith not by sight.

8. Incorporate moments of meditation or reflection in your prayers to gain insight and clarity. The world is loud. Quiet the distractions to get the attractions.
9. Follow the specific prayer rituals, postures, and timings prescribed by whatever religious tradition you find applicable. Discipline in all things keeps you in alignment.
10. A prayer a day keeps the negative away. Positive self-talk changes everything.

THE REFLECTION

What does prayer mean to you?

_____

_____

Do you believe you are praying to an outside source?

_____

_____

Name a time when a prayer request was answered.

_____

_____

CHAPTER 6

ELEVATE

Elevate:
To raise or lift something or someone to a higher position or level, either physically or metaphorically. It can refer to increasing in height, importance, status, quality, or value. In a broader sense, it implies improving or enhancing the condition or state of something or someone.

Constant elevation creates expansion.

— Rakim

THE LESSON

To elevate in the world as a spirit living this human experience, one has to understand that it will require separation from people, places, and things. One of my best friends on the planet, David Banner, told me that as my conscience and knowledge increased, the company and the frivolous conversations would decrease. Elevating on your journey doesn't mean you are better than anybody, you have just made a different decision and you have taken the proverbial "red pill." Remember, Neo had a choice. Take the red pill, embrace reality, and face the hard truths of said reality. Or take the blue pill and remain in the false, computer-generated world of the *Matrix*. Now that movie wasn't literal, but very spot-on with the overall message. We have all been lied to and indoctrinated in a false and oppressive system of tyranny and democracy that flaunts itself as fair and responsible to the people.

Once you have gotten to this point in your pedaling journey, you will no doubt experience isolation and frustration about how everyone cannot see and understand. If we all could learn the truth of the world, the world would self correct. All cultures alike would get a deeper understanding, which would create a different collective energy and we would all heal and create and do better overall. I completely feel that accountability is what the world needs the most. I personally live by the philosophy that even when it is not my fault, it is, which is another jewel from Banner. But regardless of the source, this mindset has given me so much freedom to live fully. I don't point fingers anywhere but at me. When I fuck up, I'll own it, and when I win, I'll own that too! You too can elevate yourself so you can raise your value and enhance the state or condition of your life.

THE LAWS

1. Constant elevation creates expansion, according to Rakim. Be consistent in elevating your mind, you can't help but grow.
2. Your level of success will rarely exceed your level of personal development, according to Jim Rohn. Success is an internal job.
3. The only person you are destined to become is the person you decide to be, according to Ralph Waldo Emerson We are co-creators of our lives.
4. It's not what we do once in a while that shapes our lives. It's what we do consistently, according to Tony Robbins. Keep Pedaling.
5. The biggest risk is not taking any risk. In a world that is changing quickly, the only strategy that is guaranteed to fail is not taking risks, according to Mark Zuckerberg. Every shot not taken is a miss.
6. You can be anything but not everything, according to David Allen. Focus on your focus.
7. Success is walking from failure to failure with no loss of enthusiasm,

according to Winston S. Churchill. No matter the pace, Keep Pedaling.
8. It does not matter how slowly you go, as long as you do not stop, according to Confucius. Self explanatory.
9. The only person you should try to better than is the person you were yesterday. You are your greatest asset or liability.
10. Every day just be a little better, according to Kobe Bryant. Just keep stacking days.

THE REFLECTION

From where your life is now, how many elevations can you remember?

_____

_____

Whenever you elevate or level up, do you find it lonely?

_____

_____

What part of your life do you want to elevate in?

_____

_____

CHAPTER 7

DISCIPLINE

Discipline:
Generally refers to a set of rules, practices, or behaviors that promote self-control, order, and adherence to a code of conduct. It can relate to personal self-discipline, as well as rules and expectations within organizations, institutions, or society at large. Discipline is often associated with the ability to control one's impulses, maintain consistency, and achieve goals through structured actions.

Discipline is a form of self love.

— Karon Joseph Riley

THE LESSON

Mike Tyson once said that discipline is doing something you hate like you love it because you have to. I don't necessarily believe it is exactly that. I think you will have a hard time doing anything you don't want to do if you truly hate it. I think it might be uncomfortable, you may not enjoy it, but hate is an energy that has a shelf life. There has to be some love somewhere. For me, discipline is a super power that I have. It is a gift that if I don't train at it constantly, I will fall short some days, months, or even years. When I say fall short, I say that because I have to be honest with myself. I could have had this book done three years ago, but I lacked the discipline as a writer. Now if this was something around training or getting ready for an acting role, I would have smashed it and been on my third book.

I learned a long time ago that discipline is a thing that once you know how to maintain it anywhere in your life, it is a transferable skill. If you can discipline yourself on something small, you will create the muscle you can grow and make stronger, and then you can apply that to any area of your life. This book is me growing a new muscle of discipline. When I played in the NFL, my discipline to train and not run the streets constantly is the only way I was able to play long enough to get my pension and actually gain something from the experience. I did get my streets in though. What can I say? Balance is important too. Fast forward to me transitioning to acting from pro sports. I needed to change my body to fit my new occupation of a leading man. I did the same cardio machine for two years straight. I literally went from my playing weight of 260 to 225. Now if you asked me if I loved that arch trainer machine, I would say, *Hell naw.* I did love my body changing and my new potential future. As an athlete, I've never liked running to train but I knew in order to be at my best, I had to run. So I ran. I did whatever was necessary to be what I said I was. An athlete.

It is no different now as an actor, producer, husband, and father. I confess I don't love everything about those said titles. I don't love being interrupted constantly by the inquisitive questions of a 9-year-old, but I love the fact that she is curious. So I am always available to answer her curiosity. I don't love telling my wife where I'm going or who I'm going with, but I love her and I want her to feel secure about my trust, so I protect that. I don't love sitting around on set constantly waiting but I love to play and act, so I deal with it. There are things that I loath, but I know they are necessary for me to be the best version of myself. Doing anything in the absence of love will be tough but no matter what you decide to use as your fuel source, just get it done and Keep Pedaling until you reach your goals. It is as simple as that.

THE LAWS

1. With self-discipline, most anything is possible, according to Theodore Roosevelt. It is what separates dreams from reality.
2. Discipline is the bridge between goals and accomplishment, according to Jim Rohn. Without it you just swimming in the waters of failure.
3. The ability to discipline yourself to delay gratification in the short term in order to enjoy greater rewards in the long term is the indispensable prerequisite for success, according to Brian Tracy. Not a lot of secret ingredients to winning.
4. The successful person has the habit of doing the things failures don't like to do. They don't like doing them either necessarily. But their dislike is subordinated to the strength of their purpose, according E.M. Gray. The "how" is never as important as the "why."
5. Discipline is the soul of an army. It makes small numbers formidable; procures success for the weak, and esteem to all, according to George

Washington. Discipline makes average men good and good men great.
6. Your level of success is determined by your level of discipline and perseverance. No way around it.
7. Discipline is just choosing between what you want now and what you want most. You have to be able to see around the corner.
8. The pain of discipline is far less than the pain of regret, according to Sarah Bombell. We choose which one we will live with.
9. The only discipline that lasts is self-discipline, according to Bum Phillips, because love for self should never run out.
10. Discipline is not a dirty word, according to Jack Lalanne. Another word for it is love.

THE REFLECTION

In what part of your life do you need to increase your discipline?

_____

_____

How do you avoid procrastinating on things you know you need to do?

_____

_____

Where do you think discipline will improve your life?

_____

_____

CHAPTER 8

ACCOUNTABILITY

Accountability:
Refers to the responsibility for one's actions, decisions, and the consequences that follow. It involves being answerable and transparent about one's behavior and its outcomes within personal, professional, or societal contexts. Accountability is often associated with trust, integrity, and the willingness to accept the consequences, whether positive or negative, of one's actions. It plays a crucial role in maintaining ethics, fostering transparency and ensuring that individuals and organizations are held responsible for their commitments and obligations.

It's my fault, even when it isn't.

— David Banner

THE LESSON

My best friend, David Banner, has a quote in his office that changed my life in a way that was so simple but yet so complex. The quote is, *It's my fault, even when it isn't.* If I'm being completely honest, before that moment, I had the tendency to blame others at times for things that were not going right, whether it was being late somewhere or something just not working out the way I thought it should. After I read that, my spirit completely understood it on a deep, cosmic level. So much so that I realized the power in accountability. Now I've never been a ducker of responsibility, so it wasn't hard for me to elevate and go further in my shaping of myself to be the man I aspired to be. Immediately problems in my life didn't feel like problems anymore. They felt like challenges that were mine and only mine to overcome. Nothing or no one outside of myself would get the credit for anything good or bad that happened to me. In that moment, I started to see that life happens for me and not to me. I took full control of my destiny from a spiritual and deep place. Challenges in my marriage became my fault and my challenge to own them. I owned it. Challenges in my career all became my fault. Not booking? Produce, create your own path. With this level of accountability, my favorite quote now is, *I'll own all my defeats and when I win, I'll own that too, unapologetically.* I now teach my sons and daughter this. Own your shit, and you can also own your gold. But don't go pointing fingers at nobody saying you didn't get this or that or you aren't receiving what you feel you are owed. Nobody is here to give you anything.

Your life is yours to create. Success is and will always be an inside job. In order to reach that success, whatever the field, you have to accept and own all the mistakes and challenges as your own. If I want to be hired as an actor, I have to look to create work for others and that energy comes back to me tenfold. If I want more communication with my wife, I have to communicate more and that energy comes back. If I want my kids to be leaders, I have to be a leader and by osmosis, they become leaders. You see how this works? As above, so it is below. As it is inside will be the case outside. If your life is in shambles, start inside. Find the accountability for your life being in shambles and own that. Once you can own it, you can change it. The elephant in the room only hurts you if you don't acknowledge it.

Now on the flip side, you also have to understand that bad things sometimes will happen that you don't need to make your fault. If a person was molested as a child, that was not their fault. But as an adult, it is their responsibility to seek out the proper healing of that event so that it doesn't contaminate their life. They have to take accountability for their life as an adult. When we are children, we don't have governance over ourselves yet. So accountability goes only so far. As an adult, it is all on you. Is it fair? No it's not, but it's your fault even when it isn't.

THE LAWS

1. A child who is not disciplined will not respect his elders, according to a Yoruba Proverb. Accountability starts at a young age. Without it, respect for societal norms and elders diminishes.
2. He who conceals his disease cannot be cured, according to an Ethiopian Proverb. You cannot heal what you don't reveal.
3. When there are no enemies within, the enemies outside cannot hurt you, according to an Afrikan Proverb. Internal discord or lack of self-accountability is more detrimental than external threats.
4. If you want to go fast, go alone. If you want to go far, go together, according to an Afrikan Proverb. This truth reveals that collective responsibility and teamwork are essential to lasting success.
5. A single bracelet does not jingle, according to a Congolese Proverb. Accountability is not only a personal responsibility but also a collective one.
6. Examine what is said, not he who speaks. The point is accountability

to the truth and substance over the personality.
7. The ruin of a nation begins in the homes of its people, according to an Ashanti Proverb. Take care of home before you can change the world.
8. You learn how to cut down trees by cutting down trees. Be accountable to your life experiences.
9. He who refuses to obey cannot command, according to a Kenyan Proverb. You cannot lead if you haven't taken accountability to learn how to follow.
10. Be accountable to yourself or the world will make you accountable. Get your house in order. You are not the only one that has to live in it.

THE REFLECTION

Is what area of your life do you wish you were more accountable?

_____

_____

How do you think accountability can change your perspective?

_____

_____

Does accountability scare you?

_____

_____

CHAPTER 9

LEADERSHIP

Leadership:
The act of guiding and inspiring a group of people toward achieving a common goal. It involves setting a vision, motivating and empowering team members, and making strategic decisions. Good leaders often exhibit qualities such as strong communication skills, integrity, empathy, and the ability to adapt to changing circumstances. Leadership is not just about authority. It's about fostering a collaborative environment and influencing others positively.

In order to lead, you have to know how to follow.

— Karon Joseph Riley

THE LESSON

Are leaders born or made? That is the question researchers across the globe have tried to answer. I believe it is a combination of your genetics and your environment. I believe everyone has the potential to lead in some area of their life. Maybe not the leader of a major corporation but hey, some folks rock at organizing a party but would totally bomb if they had to run a company. The traits that all leaders have is positive energy and the capacity to go-go-go with a healthy vigor and upbeat attitude through good times and bad; the ability to energize others, releasing their positive energy to take any hill; and the ability to make tough choices with yes or no, not maybe. They have the talent to execute and last but never lose passion. They have to care deeply. I also think emotional intelligence is huge.

At this point in my life, I can say I have all of these traits. Can I say I was born with these? To a degree, I say yes. I also say that without proper guidance, resources, and life training, all of these traits would not have manifested to create the leader I am today. I had the good fortune of being born into a family where I was first and second at the same time. I was my father's first-born son and my mother's second-born son, which I believe was crucial in my development. I learned the ability to lead and follow at the same time. Your life circumstances will play a part in the outcome of your life. I say that to explain that you don't have to have ideal circumstances to lead. You just need to understand that somebody has to. I have no problem following if there is a stronger leader in the mix. If there isn't anyone stronger, I have zero problems stepping into the leadership role.

Knowing how to lead and follow requires the absence of ego. As I've grown, I've learned to accept that in most situations, I'll take the lead. I prefer it. They say in cycling, the safest place in the peloton is in the front or the very back, never in the middle. The middle is the most dangerous. From the front, you control the pace and are ahead of the accidents unless you cause one yourself. At the very back, you risk the chance of being left but you can see everyone ahead and if there is a crash, you can see it and hopefully avoid it. When I take my kids to school, I say three things to them every time: *Have a great day, I love you, and be a leader.* In my mind, I am programming my kids to not ever look to follow anyone but instead rely on their own intuition. Then if any crashes occur, it is by their own doing, which in essence is the universe happening for them. They will naturally learn to follow by my leadership, but one day they will have to on their own. So leadership is a key component to everyone's journey. It may present itself in different arenas, but you have to have the ability to lead somewhere or you will get taken anywhere.

THE LAWS

1. The greatest leader is not necessarily the one who does the greatest things. He is the one that gets the people to do the greatest things, according to President Ronald Reagan. Being a leader is more about inspiring than anything.
2. Management is doing right. Leadership is doing the right things, according to Peter Drucker. Your integrity has to be unmatched.
3. A leader is one who knows the way, goes the way, and shows the way, according to Peter Drucker, which is showing and proving.
4. Leadership is not about titles, positions, or flowcharts. It is about life influencing another, according to John C. Maxwell. Service to others is our rent here on earth.
5. The best leaders are those most interested in surrounding themselves with assistants and associates smarter than they are, according to John Wooden. Good leaders think it's about them. Great leaders know it isn't.

6. To handle yourself, use your head. To handle others, use your heart, according to Eleanor Roosevelt. Things are to be used, not people.
7. Leadership is the capacity to translate vision into reality, according to Warren Bennis. You have to be able to see around the corner.
8. A genuine leader is not a searcher for consensus but a molder of consensus, according to Martin Luther King Jr. You have to mold the clay you have.
9. The quality of a leader is reflected in the standards they set for themselves, according to Ray Kroc, and also by the circle they keep.
10. Leadership is not about being in charge. It is about taking care of those in your charge, according to Simon Sinek. The people you do it for should be who is in charge.

THE REFLECTION

Who in your life would you consider a great leader? Why?

_____

_____

Have you ever had to lead a group of people?

_____

_____

Would you trust yourself to lead yourself? Why or why not?

_____

_____

CHAPTER 10

INTEGRITY

Integrity:
Refers to the quality of being honest and having strong moral principles. It involves being consistent in actions, values, methods, measures, principles, expectations, and outcomes. A person with integrity acts according to a set of ethical and moral principles and does not veer from them, even in private. It often entails doing the right thing, even when no one is watching, and upholding ethical standards in both personal and professional life. Integrity is fundamental to trust and credibility in all aspects of life.

I walk into every room as myself.

— Jay Z

THE LESSON

This part of the Keep Pedaling mantra is the easiest and hardest action. I say that because integrity could be called bravery in some circles, bravery to be your full self in your truth and stand on that no matter the circumstances. What makes bravery hard is that it isn't the absence of fear, it is the ability to move forward despite that fear. Telling the truth to your parents, girlfriend, teacher, coach, husband, wife, or friend requires you have the bravery despite the fact that said truth could create an uncomfortable environment for all included. Or it could leave you open and vulnerable. It becomes easier to be brave if you have worked on the first nine pillars.

When I was a young boy and man, I would lie to keep everything peaceful, more so for myself, which was selfish. As I've grown and matured and the mantra became the man, I no longer feel the need to adjust my truth for anybody's comfort, mine included. I say mine because even in living in my full authenticity, the times when I put myself out there are truly still scary. Each time I do, it gets less scary. I get braver and more accountable to myself and my truth. When I was younger, my truth was what my parents, world, or a person male or female told me it was. I was operating based on everyone's opinion of me other than my own. Once I unlearned a lot of the things this world had force fed me and started to do the work on myself, I found I gained strength in not listening to anybody about my narrative. I learned that any opinion outside of self is just noise. This way of living and operating has gained me a level of peace that I wish upon you as you read this and learn how to open up your internal pedaler. Then you can see that standing on your integrity will at times be uncomfortable, but in that discomfort will always come growth and understanding.

There was a period in my marriage where it seemed all was lost, but my wife and I took a course through Landmark, which focuses on each person showing up in their full authentic self regardless of what anybody else thought about it. I recommend anybody struggling with being brave enough to live in their authenticity to look into the Landmark program. I'm not getting a kick back for promoting this program, I truly just want folks to get out of their own way. I truly believe if we all focus on ourselves that this world will self-correct and we can then truly be a society that respects each other's cultures and communities and it isn't a problem.

In conclusion, your integrity will become your signature of life. It will be incorporated in that dash between the day you are born and the day you leave here. I implore you to work toward living your full truth and allow your integrity to proceed your arrival into any room on the planet.

THE LAWS

1. Honesty is the first chapter in the book of wisdom, according to an Afrikan Proverb. Truth of self is always first.
2. Truth does not spoil over time, according to an Afrikan Proverb. Once true it will always be.
3. A clear conscience fears no accusation, according to an Afrikan Proverb. When you stay in your truth and act so, no pointing fingers can scare you.
4. Your beauty cannot serve the world. Integrity goes deeper than superficial.
5. He who earns calamity, eats it with his family, according to an Afrikan Proverb, which reveals the consequence of not having integrity.
6. The mouth which eats does not talk, according to a Congolese Proverb, which reveals that the virtue of integrity means fulfilling one's duties quietly and without boasting.
7. The beauty of a man is in his integrity and his ability to affect those around him positively, according to an Afrikan Proverb. The true beauty of anyone resides in their acceptance of their truth.

8. When you follow the path of your father, you learn to walk like him, according to an Ashanti Proverb. This truth shows the importance of role models having integrity.
9. An upright man can be counted on. He does not veer away, according to an Afrikan Proverb. It means something when people can count on you.
10. Money can't talk, yet it can make lies look true, according to a South Afrikan Proverb. Don't let money corrupt your values or your integrity.

THE REFLECTION

Are you truthful about who you're with people, or do you present a representative?

_____

_____

Can you be counted on to do what you said you would do?

_____

_____

Do you believe your own truth?

_____

_____

CHAPTER 11

NAVIGATE

Navigate:
To plan and direct the course of a journey, particularly by using maps or instruments, such as in the context of sailing, driving, or walking. In a broader sense, it can also refer to the process of managing one's way through or dealing with a complex situation or system. This could include navigating through complex information, social situations, or organizational structures. The term encapsulates both the physical act of moving through spaces and the metaphorical act of maneuvering through various aspects of life or work.

Going in the right direction doesn't always mean you are on the right path.

— Afrikan Proverb

THE LESSON

I love the quote, *A smooth sea has never made a skilled sailor*. The reality of that statement is that none of us walking this planet will get out without all of the necessary lessons needed to become a skilled sailor. I know I have had my rough seas, and I have become a pretty good sailor out here in this ocean of life we live in. I believe I have avoided some storms by heeding some of the signs that the most high (universe) sent me. And I'm thankful for my intuitive connection to spirit. That intuition has served me well by helping me find my renewed spiritual connection through the Yoruba of West Africa. They study the IFA (Orisha) and pay homage to the most high Oludumare. Now this book isn't about religion, but it is very much about spirit. The mantra once practiced will give you the ability to become a skilled sailor in this ocean of life. I'm thankful for the self-knowledge I have gained because with every new door opened, the universe sent something to fill it up with purpose.

Now in this portion of the mantra, navigating becomes paramount to one's very survival and will determine the life you have. Let's unpack the very definition of navigate. The first line of the definition given above speaks of a journey and navigating the journey using maps or instruments. I think we can all agree that this life we all have is like our own journeys in their own right. I connected it to navigating as if sailing in the ocean. I've always had a fantasy of sailing the open seas with all the adventure and danger that comes. In my life, Keep Pedaling has been my map that I have developed over time. I didn't even know I had it until I had it. It came to me on my bike one day.

The definition also speaks of managing one's way through or dealing with complex situations or systems. As long as you have your guidance system up-to-date, you will be able to deal with all the different situations or systems presented to you. I truly hope up to this point in the book you see how this mantra, when broken down, can definitely give you a guidepost for life.

The last part of the navigation definition states that the term encapsulates both the physical act of moving through spaces and the metaphorical act of maneuvering through various aspects of life or work. Whether you see your life as a metaphorical ship or bike, get you a mission statement that you can refer to for help when the seas or road get undoubtedly hard. Here is mine, and you are welcome to it. Whatever you do, just Keep Pedaling.

THE LAWS

1. The pessimist complains about the wind. The optimist expects it to change. The realist adjusts the sails, according to William Arthur Ward. Don't complain, adjust.
2. You can't change the direction of the wind, but you can adjust your sails to always reach your destination, according to Jimmy Dean. You must have the ability to pivot.
3. It is not the ship so much as the skillful sailing that assures the prosperous voyage, according to George William Curtis. Situations change. You gotta stay solid.
4. Life is like sailing. You can use any wind to go in any direction, according to Robert Brault. Life happens for you, not to you.
5. The art of life is a constant readjustment to our surroundings, according to Kakuzo Okakura. Constant elevation creates expansion.
6. I am not afraid of storms for I am learning how to sail my ship, according to Louisa May Alcott. It is all serving your purpose. Embrace it.

7. He who is outside his door has the hardest part of his journey behind him, according to a Dutch Proverb. Just get home.
8. To reach a port, we must sail, sometimes with the wind, and sometimes against it. But we must not drift or lie at anchor, according to Oliver Wendell Holmes Sr. Slow progress isn't the crime, no progress is.
9. In the middle of every difficulty lies opportunity, according to Albert Einstein. Struggle is necessary for growth.
10. No matter what happens, or how bad it seems today, life does go on, and it will be better tomorrow, according to Maya Angelou. Keep Pedaling.

THE REFLECTION

What skills do you need to acquire or strengthen to guide your journey?

_____

_____

What do you need to become a skilled sailor of life?

_____

_____

How do you find your way back during those times when you feel lost in life?

_____

_____

CHAPTER 12

GIVE

Give:
To freely transfer possession of something to someone else, without expecting anything in return. For example, giving a gift to a friend.

To give is better than to receive.

— Quote unknown

THE LESSON

The great Muhammed Ali once said that our service to others is the rent we pay for our room here on earth. This quote highlights Ali's belief of the importance of helping and serving others as a fundamental responsibility and purpose in life. It reflects his commitment to humanitarian efforts and his perspective to the significance of giving back to the community and the world at large. I too have grown to feel the same way. I developed this feeling after playing the Champ in a feature film called *The Last Punch*. While working as an actor to embody Ali's spirit, I discovered what really made him tick as a man. The bravado and belief in his people was his gift back to his people. That is why G is for give.

Once you start to find your way on this journey by navigating into relatively smooth seas of life, it is your responsibility and mine to give the game back. Universal intelligence is accessible to all, but some are able to tap into it more freely. Like an alchemist, I consider myself one of the people who understands this and believes I have access to the Universal wisdom. In order to keep access, I cannot withhold it from another traveler who may be looking for a map to navigate this thing called life.

I've lived a pretty amazing life up to this point, and it's only getting better because I am constantly pedaling, constantly looking to evolve and gain wisdom so I can be of service to my people. To give is the greatest thing we can do. Every one of us has genius ability in some area of life. It is our responsibility to find what that is and then help others find theirs. While doing this for others, never forget to give yourself knowledge of self and experiences to help you evolve and find your purpose. Give yourself time to pray to elevate and the discipline to be accountable and to lead with integrity, all while navigating your journey. This is truly my belief.

So I give you my mantra, my code, my way of life, my map in this truly amazing ocean of life. A map to keep with you whether you are on a bike, plane, or simply walking. The only rule is to Keep Pedaling!

THE LAWS

1. The hand that gives, gathers. This is the idea that generosity benefits both the giver and the receiver, creating a cycle of abundance.
2. If you think you are too small to make a difference, you haven't spent the night with a mosquito. This proverb suggests that even the smallest act of giving or contribution can have a significant impact.
3. One who eats alone cannot discuss the taste of the food with others. This proverb suggests that sharing experiences, including giving, enriches life.
4. A kind gesture can reach a wound that only compassion can heal. This emphasizes the power of giving not just in material terms but with acts of kindness and empathy.
5. When you give a grain of rice to a child, you feed another child's heart. This illustrates the ripple effect of giving, especially in the context of community and nurturing the young.
6. He who gives early gives twice. This implies that timely assistance or giving is more valuable and impactful.

7. A generous man will always be prosperous. This proverb underscores the belief that generosity leads to abundance and prosperity in various forms.
8. Give little by little, and even a small amount will grow. This Afrikan Proverb emphasizes the importance of consistent giving, no matter how small the contribution. Over time, modest acts of generosity can accumulate and lead to significant outcomes.
9. We desire to bequeath two things to our children. The first one is roots, the other one is wings. This proverb from Sudan is about giving the next generation both stability and the freedom to explore.
10. The meaning of life is to find your gift. The purpose of life is to give it away, according to Pablo Picasso.

THE REFLECTION

Have you ever given without looking for something in return? What was the result?

_____

_____

In what ways has this book helped you in understanding yourself?

_____

_____

Will you give the game back by recommending this book to a wayward traveler of life?

_____

_____

PERSONAL QUOTES

The following is a list of my personal, internal quotes that I came up with over time, most often while riding my bike.

"No matter how long it takes,
just Keep Pedaling."

"Proper communication requires
the right source and filter."

"Your dreams are like your mortgage
or your car note. It ain't really yours
until you pay off your debt. Don't let
anyone or anything outwork you for it."

"Start with grateful and end with
grateful, and everything in the
middle stays in its place."

"When a man can be honest
with his weaknesses, he can be
bold with his strengths."

"Self-discipline and self-love
are the same thing."

"Be vigilant with whom you share your dreams and energy with." "Average is a mentality, and so is greatness. Choose wisely."

"Your past should inform your future decisions, but only if you see your past with truthful eyes."

"If it scares you, run toward it. That is the sweet spot of where growth and life meet."

"Nothing on this planet has grown with darkness."

"Hard work ensures victory, no matter the outcome."

"Regret and gratitude are like oil and water. They can coexist, but they will never mix."

"A man or woman with a plan is hard to defeat, but a man or a woman who is working that plan is undefeated."

MY PELOTON (MY VILLAGE)

Peloton by definition is the main field or group of cyclists in a race. In the context I'm using, Peloton is my circle of friends, my village. Here are a series of quotes from my group of brothers and sisters from other misters who are in this race of life with me, and at times have helped me save energy and have helped me to ride faster or slower depending on the situation. These are some of their rules they live by.

DAVID BANNER

David is one of my closest friends in the world. He is a Grammy-nominated rapper, entrepreneur, producer, activist, and all around amazing brother to me and many others.

"It's my fault, even when it isn't."

LEM COLLINS

Lem is another one of my dearest friends and my business partner with our production company Dedicated Prophecy Films, LLC. Lem is also an actor, producer, writer, director, painter, and the keeper of the faith for our crew.

"Superior men do superior man shit."

"I play chess, never checkers."

ERROL SADLER

Producer, father, brother, friend, business partner, and a great man.

"If I call you brother, then I want for you all that I have and more."

"Don't call me brother if you don't wish upon me the same level of success that you have."

"Don't call me brother if you have the answers to my problems but choose to keep a closed mouth."

"Don't call me a brother if you know that my steps are out of alignment, mortally, spiritually, and ethically, and you don't hold me accountable."

KEITH NEAL

Producer, ex-NFL receiver, co-founder of Swirlfilms, father, mentor, brother.

"Respect is king."

"If you have respect for God, your days will be longer and your life will be rich."

"If you respect money, you will always have a dollar."

"If you respect love, your heart will be full and your actions will be just."

"If you respect others, others will respect you, and respect encompasses ALL things."

BRYAN SCOTT

Best friend, brother, son, husband, father, ex-NFL cornerback, entrepreneur, one of the best men I know, period. And a surrogate little bro.

"Just because you can doesn't mean you should."

JIMMI SANDERS

Childhood best friend, one of the original brothers off the block. Father, son, coach, hustler for the community. Never wished another man bad times.

"You are the five closest people to you."

"All ships must sail in the same direction in order to do anything significant."

BERNARD ROBERTSON

Best friend, brother, son, husband, father, ex-NFL lineman, money manager, partner of Hackett Robertson group, and an amazing man I'm proud to call brother.

Proverbs 4: 5-9:

Get wisdom, get understanding: forget it not; neither decline from the words of my mouth. Forsake her not, and she shall preserve thee: love her, and she shall keep thee. Wisdom is the principal thing; therefore get wisdom: and with all thy getting, get understanding. Exalt her, and she shall bring thee to honor, when thou dost embrace her.

She shall give to thine head an ornament of grace: a crown of glory shall she deliver to thee.

VINCE SANTANA

A brother to me and mine, father, husband, financial guru, the one man who put it on the line for me. Executive producer for my production company.

> *"I trust everybody to be the person they have shown to be."*
>
> *"Men have a role, women have a role. The roles are not the same."*
>
> *"A man's loyalty to his woman is not the same as a woman's loyalty to a man."*

RYAN LAMONT JONES

Mentor, leader, father, husband, author, teacher, speaker, damn good brother I am proud to know.

> *"The only people who are qualified to reign with you are the people who stood in the rain with you."*
>
> *"Everyone in your circle is not in your corner."*
>
> *"Proximity is power: Always remember that who you spend the most time with is who you eventually become. The people in my corner (bullseye circle), are the chosen and the golden ones. They literally hold*

me down, always support me without me having to ask, and offer their assistance to further develop me and my business. They are the ones that when push comes to shove, they will always have my back. They are my warriors on the battlefield."

"The people on the outer bullseye circle are the ones that might cheer you on while you are on the battlefield, but they are definitely not jumping in it to help you win."

LAMAR "MARVL" WEST

My brother as far as I'm concerned, father, brother, son, dopest camera operator, best friend, my consistent six-keeper, and baseball aficionado.

"Always go home, A man's home is HIS space."

"Use your space young man. Home is where you rest, relax, plan, and reign no matter what. As a leader of your family, it's where you have to be. Always go home. It needs you as much as you need it."

DEREK RUSSO

Actor, athlete, father, and damn good man.

"When you apologize, look the person in the eye."

"Your past doesn't dictate your future."

"Respect is earned."

JIMMY FARRIS

Best friend, ex-NFL receiver, Super Bowl champ, motivational speaker, author, pilot, the coolest white guy I know, and another one of my brothers from another mother.

"Always be prepared. If you stay ready, you don't have to get ready. Proper preparation prevents poor performance."

"Sweat the small stuff. Details matter. It's usually the Is you didn't dot or the Ts you didn't cross that trip you up. The best of the best sweat the details."

FRED RILEY JR.

My father, educator, counselor, brother, son, grandfather, my first hero, always my #1 guy, and a true renaissance man.

"When you meet someone, always make and hold eye contact, and always give them a firm handshake. When you say your name, say the first and last name loud and clear."

DJ SHOKLEY

Ex-NFL quarterback, sportscaster, husband, father, and one helluva brother.

> *"If you want to look good in front of thousands, you have to outwork thousands in front of nobody."*

> *"Don't care how tall your father is. You have to do your own growing."*

WAYNE OVERSTREET

Editor extraordinaire, CEO of Go Media Productions, friend, husband, father, brother, and one of the most sincere men I've met.

> *"Give thanks and praise to the Creator in all that you do."*

> *"Always ask the Creator for the words to say, the ability to listen, the wisdom to make the right decision, and that His will be done before doing anything."*

> *"Take time to make memories because when you're older, you won't remember the money and deals but the times and moments."*

"Be humble or be humbled."

COACH WES LEE

Actor, singer, life coach, teacher, husband, friend to me, and one of the most talented people I've ever met—and I've met a lot of talented people.

"Only results matter."

"Get your mind right and control your thoughts because what you think of will manifest."

"Think through anything you say or do because there is nothing you can say or do to take back anything you say or do."

GEORGE PIERRE

Casting director, husband, father, friend, son, and by far one of the coolest dudes in the industry.

"It's not that I think I'm better than you, I'm just a better version of what I used to be."

JAY MORRISON

Founder of Tulsa Real Estate Fund, activist, brother, husband, father, son, and one of my dearest friends who I consider a brother in my village.

> *"Men do what they have to do.*
> *Boys do what they want to do."*

JOMO HANKERSON

My big brother, my first bar and protector, a father, son, CEO, genius, one of the smartest and most giving people I know, and Angelia's firstborn.

> *"Once you make it to the one*
> *percent once, every other time*
> *after that is muscle memory."*

RODERICK MINGER

Comedian, actor, writer, husband, friend, and one of my closest friends in the entertainment world, always solid, always true.

"I listen to understand, not to respond."

" I don't follow trends. I live by my own."

" I move on logic, never emotion,
I don't care who I'm talking to."

BENNY WHITE

Basketball coach, husband, father, and leader of men. One of the best men I have ever known, I hold him responsible for helping me see my true self, which helped me become the man I am today. He also helped me be a damn good basketball player.

> *"Treat others as you would want them to treat you and or family."*
>
> *"Remember to ask a man how his family and business are doing."*

KEON HENDERSON

First best friend in life, first person I ever got into a fight with, and my brother from another mother. He is a man I've always loved and is a father, son, and loyal friend.

> *"If they don't give you a seat at the table, bring a folding chair."*
>
> *"Not everything faced can be changed, but nothing can be changed until it is faced."*
>
> *"I respect the women on this earth because they are the keys to the car. My kids keep my gas tank full and my heart full of love so I can perform my daily life."*

MR. CHARLES DAVID MOODY

Founder and CEO of C.D. Moody Construction, a husband, father, PaPa, mentor, and one of the coolest, wisest men I know and respect.

"I only leave the house to make money."

"Turn trauma into triumph."

APOSTLE JAMIE PLEASANT

Pastor, friend, husband, father, mentor, professor, and a true man of God who I love and respect to the utmost.

"Success doesn't happen overnight, but one night success happens."

TERRI J. VAUGHN RILEY

My wife, my partner, the best teammate I've ever had, the mother of my legacy, one of the most beautiful spirits I've had the privilege to know, my lover and my love.

"Be kind. Be present. Enjoy the moment."

"Laughter is healing."

"She believed she could, so she did."

EPILOGUE

As we wrap up *Keep Pedaling: The Things I Learned on My Bike*, my hope is that you overstand and innerstand exactly what it means when you hear me tell folks to Keep Pedaling. It is my way of saying to you that you matter and your dreams matter. It is my way of sending energy to all that matters to you, and for you to know that your life destiny is an inside job. Whatever you shall see inside can be manifested outside. I am proud of you. Asè! Keep Pedaling!

ACKNOWLEDGMENTS

First and foremost, I want to thank my Creator and my parents, Fred and Angelia Riley. My village of aunts, uncles, and family friends who poured into me and my family. To my ancestors, Angelia, Aretta, Thelma, Loraine, Logan, Earlene, Fred Sr., Mildred, Paul Sr., Paul Jr., and everyone I don't know by name. Without those who came before me, I would not know where to pick up. I want to say thank you to every teacher, coach, mentor, friend, and/or enemy who has taught me something through either knowledge or experience. To my wife, Terri J. Vaughn-Riley, I chose the right woman for this journey to evolve and grow. You have taught me what unconditional love is. I hope I have served you just as well. Let us keep growing, loving, and pedaling. To my children, Daylen, Kal'El, and Lola, my constant whys when the world doesn't make sense. You will always be my compass to get back to the foundation of me, and you will remain some of my greatest teachers. Keep Pedaling.

ADDITIONAL ACKNOWLEDGMENTS

Beverly Hightower, Lantz Hightower, Glenn Hightower, Chaka Hightower, Brittany Hightower, Lantz Hightower Jr., Jomo Hankerson, Jabruan Riley, Paul Hamilton lll, Shanga Hankerson, Lynette Barnes, Reggie Barnes, Jay Griffin, Lorna Gambrell, Brandon Gambrell, Shelby Gambrell, Ayodele Oyinsan, Walter Lungsford, Omari Lewis, Antonio Enoex, Jimmi Sanders, Edkar McBurrows, Anthony Thompson, Curtis Blackwell, Keyonte Wilson, Cecil Forbes, Deon Hunt, Dwayne Gwinner, Norman Clements, Claude Jerdine, James Theus, Jason Pitts, Sterling Anderson, Greg Anderson, Coach Harvell, Coach Tracey, Benny White, Duran Walker, Cookie Marsh, James Reynolds, Leonard Cry, Kevin Shephard, Alozo Littlejohn, "Big Lou" Luthor Campbell, Mrs. Merriweather, Mrs. Sadler,

Miss Susan Watson, Veda Sharp, Kenneth Sharp, Byron Ruffin, Jerry Payne, Nkumu Mandugu, Jay Harvey, Tyree Taylor, Kenneth Imo, Mercury Hall, Jason Evans, Jack Brewer, Antoine Henderson, Curtis Poole, Grant Carter, Thomas Tapeh, Terrence Floyd, Elvin Jones, Ron Johnson, Anthony "Spice" Adams, Connie "Ma Spice" Adams, Judy Elston, Daune Elston Sr., Elvin Jones, Ron Johnson, Anthony "Spice" Adams, Helen Vaughn, Milton Vaughn, Jovell Jones, Tiffany West, Marvel West, Eric Lowry, Dwayne Lowry, Nikita Lowry, Keon Henderson, Wanda Shelley, Bryan Scott, Jimmy Farris, Brandon Scott, Kimberly Scott, Miesha Scott, David Banner, Roderick Minger, Jasmine Minger, Emanuel Johnson, Rahman Mosby, April Mosby, Sean Bennett, Aquilla Bennett, Ashari Hankerson, Jomo Hankerson Jr., Heather Wesley, Mr. Charles David Moody, Apostle Jamie Pleasant, Kimberly Pleasant, Keith Neal, Tyler Perry, Peter Wise, Will Packer, Kim Fields, Chip Fields, Errol Sadler, Devon Smith, Mark Snyder, David Gibbs, Tasha Smith, Sara Mornell, Ernestine Morrison, Tequilla Whitfield, Solomon Wiliams, Latonya Wilder, Sheree Gardner, Kathryn Williams, Yvette Williams, Lyani Powers, Nykesha

Sales, Alexis Johnson, Dorsey Levens, Tiffany Brown, Chanita Foster, Roderick Minger, Clayton Landy, Lauren Darden, Alton Darden, Kikora Dorsey, Jimmy Hammond, Pat Hammond, Nicole Ari Parker, Boris Kodjoe, Malinda Williams, Tyreke Walker, Tamara Bass, Cass Sigers, Donna Permell, and the teachers and staff at Hampton Elementary, Halley Middle School, and Martin Luther King, Jr. Senior High School.

ABOUT THE AUTHOR

Karon Joseph Riley is a father, husband, brother, friend, mentor, actor, producer, director, athlete, Pan-Africanist, author, and spirit living a human existence the best way he can remember. Born and raised in Detroit, Michigan, to two educators who helped him find his path early on, Karon is a graduate of the University of Minnesota and Martin Luther King, Jr. Senior High School. He played seven years of professional football with the NFL, CFL, and AFL.

After finishing one dream as a professional athlete, Karon set his sights on the next dream of becoming an actor. He has devoted his life to living up to the responsibility of the Talented Tenth and leading the way with his gift of creativity to change the world for the better. Even as a child, Karon prayed for wisdom above all else. With a life in which he has so far lived out every dream, he has undoubtedly been blessed with wisdom along the journey. He believes that all information is a part of the universal consciousness and belongs to no single person. This book is him returning the consciousness back to keep the flow of life moving and him living his purpose.

Karon has three children, Daylen, Kal'El, and Lola, with his wife, Terri J. Vaughn Riley.

ADD YOUR OWN LAWS

ADD YOUR OWN LAWS

_____

_____

_____

_____

_____

_____

_____

_____

_____

_____

ADD YOUR OWN LAWS

Milton Keynes UK
Ingram Content Group UK Ltd.
UKHW022118220724
445848UK00012B/169